The Greatest Gymnast of All

WORLD CHAMP

by Stuart J. Murphy • illustrated by Cynthia Jabar

LEVEL 1

To Ronne Hartfield—
the greatest enthusiast of all
—S.J.M.

For my gymnastic nieces
Fiona, Ehrica, Marcie, Laura, and Emily
—C.J.

The illustrations for this book were done with acrylic paint on 140 lb. Arches hot press watercolor paper.

HarperCollins®, ◼®, and MathStart® are trademarks of HarperCollins Publishers Inc.
For more information about the MathStart series, please write to
HarperCollins Children's Books, 10 East 53rd Street, New York, NY 10022,
or visit our web site at http://www.harperchildrens.com.

Bugs incorporated in the MathStart series design were painted by Jon Buller.

Library of Congress Cataloging-in-Publication Data
Murphy, Stuart J., date
   The greatest gymnast of all / by Stuart J. Murphy ; illustrated by Cynthia Jabar.
      p.   cm.   (MathStart)
   "Level 1."
   Summary: While performing an energetic gymnastic routine, Zoe demonstrates such spatial opposites as on and off, inside and outside, and over and under.
      ISBN 0-06-027608-8. — ISBN 0-06-027609-6 (lib. bdg.) — ISBN 0-06-446718-X (pbk.)
   1. Geometry—Juvenile literature.   2. Polarity—Juvenile literature.   [1. Geometry.   2. Polarity.   3. English language—synonyms and antonyms.]   I. Jabar, Cynthia, ill.   II. Title.   III. Series.
QA445.5.M86   1998   97-51273
516—DC21   CIP
                                                                                                                  AC

Typography by Elynn Cohen and Christine Casarsa
5   6   7   8   9   10
❖

The Greatest Gymnast of All

I swing. I jump. And then I shout,
"This is what I'm all about!"
I'm ZIPPING, ZOOMING ZOE—
the greatest gymnast of all.

I cartwheel on,

then off the mat.

My leaps are short,
or **long**—like that.

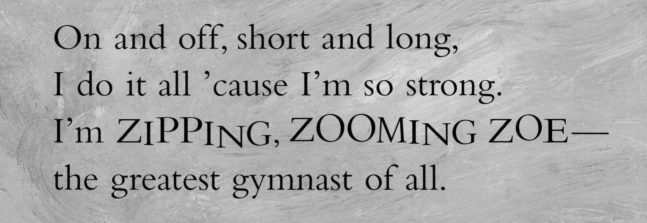

On and off, short and long,
I do it all 'cause I'm so strong.
I'm ZIPPING, ZOOMING ZOE—
the greatest gymnast of all.

Inside the hoop

and outside then.

I'm over the hoop,

and under again.

15

Inside, outside, over and under.
I think that I am truly a wonder.
I'm ZIPPING, ZOOMING ZOE—
the greatest gymnast of all.

A forward roll,

18

A backward flip.

I'm high—
then low.

I rarely slip.

21

Forward, backward, high and low.
I'm putting on a wonderful show.
I'm ZIPPING, ZOOMING ZOE—
the greatest gymnast of all.

I swing way up,

24

and down below.

My feet are near.

Out far they go.

Up and down, near and far.
I feel like I'm a superstar.

I'm ZIPPING, ZOOMING ZOE—
the greatest gymnast of all.

If you would like to have more fun with the math concepts presented in *The Greatest Gymnast of All*, here are a few suggestions:

- Read the story with the child and describe what is going on in each picture.

- Throughout the story, ask questions about Zoe's positions, such as: "Where is Zoe?" and "Where is she now?" and "Is she over or under the hoop?"

- Encourage the child to tell the story using his or her own words.

- Introduce the concept of opposites. For example, say, "Near and far go together because they are opposites." "If I say big, what is the opposite?" "Can you think of some opposites?"

- Find some household items that represent opposites. Sit in a big chair and then a small one. Point out something placed high in the refrigerator and an item that is low. Discover other opposites together.

- Look at things outside the home—at the playground, during a trip to the zoo, or in your neighborhood—and identify the opposites. Ask questions such as: "Are some kids at the top of the slide and some at the bottom?" "Which animals are tall and which are short?" "Are some trees near the house and some far away?"

Following are some activities that will help you extend the concepts presented in *The Greatest Gymnast of All* into a child's everyday life.

Taking a Bath: Discuss all the opposites that can be found while taking a bath. Ask questions such as: "When is the bathtub full, and when is it empty?" "Is the water hot or cold?" Practice turning the water faucet on and off. Describe hair, toys, or washcloths that are dry or wet, long or short, big or small.

Going for a Walk: Go for a stroll in the neighborhood and point out opposites. "Are there many cars parked on the street or just a few?" "What moves slowly and what moves quickly?" "Which store is near our house and which store is far away?"

Acting the Part: Ask each family member to pick a set of opposites and act them out. Have the rest of the family guess what the opposites are.

The following stories include similar concepts to those that are presented in *The Greatest Gymnast of All*:

- EXACTLY THE OPPOSITE by Tana Hoban

- TRAFFIC: A BOOK OF OPPOSITES by Betsy and Giulio Maestro

- BECCA BACKWARD, BECCA FORWARD by Bruce McMillan